The Story
of the
WEST
HIGHLAND

*The 1940's LNER guide to the
West Highland Railway reprinted*

Famedram Publishers, Gartocharn

Reprinted by Famedram Publishers, Gartocharn by kind permission of
the British Railways Board. Original copies of the 1944 and 1947 editions were loaned by
the West Highland Museum, Fort William.

CONTENTS

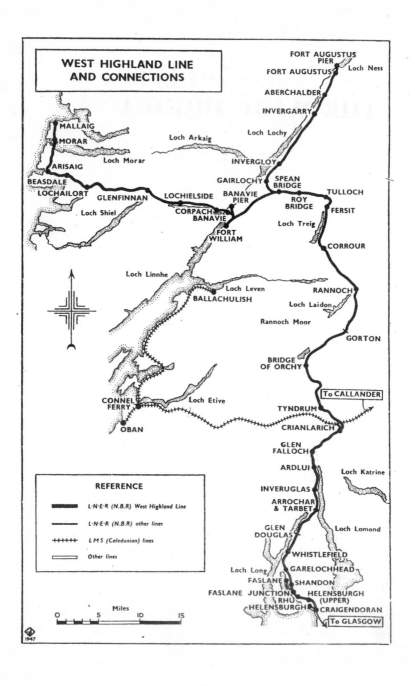

WEST HIGHLAND LINE
AND CONNECTIONS

FORT AUGUSTUS PIER
FORT AUGUSTUS
Loch Ness
ABERCHALDER
INVERGARRY
Loch Lochy
MALLAIG
MORAR
Loch Arkaig
INVERGLOY
ARISAIG
Loch Morar
GAIRLOCHY
SPEAN BRIDGE
BEASDALE
LOCHAILORT
GLENFINNAN
LOCHIELSIDE
BANAVIE PIER
ROY BRIDGE
TULLOCH
FERSIT
Loch Shiel
CORPACH
BANAVIE
FORT WILLIAM
Loch Treig
CORROUR
Loch Linnhe
Loch Leven
BALLACHULISH
RANNOCH
Loch Laidon
Rannoch Moor
GORTON
BRIDGE OF ORCHY
To CALLANDER
CONNEL FERRY
Loch Etive
TYNDRUM
OBAN
CRIANLARICH
GLEN FALLOCH
ARDLUI
Loch Katrine
INVERUGLAS
ARROCHAR & TARBET
Loch Lomond
GLEN DOUGLAS
WHISTLEFIELD
GARELOCHHEAD
Loch Long
FASLANE
SHANDON
FASLANE JUNCTION
HELENSBURGH (UPPER)
RHU
HELENSBURGH
CRAIGENDORAN
To GLASGOW

REFERENCE

L·N·E·R (N.B.R) West Highland Line

L·N·E·R (N.B.R) other lines

+++++ L M S (Caledonian) lines

Other lines

Miles

0   5   10   15

1947

THE STORY OF
THE WEST HIGHLAND

I—HISTORICAL SURVEY

" I am aware that many people nowadays regard the train as the second-best means of seeing a country. In Scotland, at any rate, that notion can be cherished to the point of prejudice. We have, indeed, several stretches of line which in scenic outlook are immeasurably richer than the roads leading to the same destinations, and one of them is the West Highland Railway." Thus wrote J. J. Bell in *The Glory of Scotland* of one of the boldest railway engineering projects ever to be accomplished in Great Britain, and of which the original section from Craigendoran to Fort William completed the fiftieth year of its existence on 7th August 1944.

The origin of the West Highland dates back to 1884, when an independent company styled the Glasgow & North Western Railway, and backed by the North British Railway, was formed to build a line from the latter at Maryhill in Glasgow to Fort William via Strathblane, Drymen, the eastern side of Loch Lomond, Crianlarich, Tyndrum, Rannoch Moor and Glencoe to Loch Leven, which was to be crossed near Ballachulish, thence along the coast through Onich. But this was not all. It was also planned to continue the line through the Great Glen to connect with the Highland Railway some five miles south of Inverness. Had the scheme been carried through the Glasgow & North Western would have brought Inverness within 160 miles of Glasgow by rail, 47 miles nearer than by the existing route of the Caledonian and Highland Railways via Perth, and when the Bill came before Parliament the Highland naturally fought it tooth and nail.

Although the Highland Railway was successful in getting the Bill rejected, the project was revived in another form three years later. This time the line through the Great Glen was omitted and, under the title of the West Highland Railway, a Bill was introduced into Parliament to build a line from Helensburgh on the North British to Fort William via Loch Lomond, Rannoch Moor and Spean Bridge. Originally it had been intended to carry the line through to Roshven, some 15 miles short of Mallaig, but owing to the strong opposition of the landowners, the Fort William-Roshven section was vetoed. The Highland again opposed the

The big moment – official opening, Fort William, August 11, 1894.

scheme, but without success, for the Act was passed on 12th August 1889. In the following session Parliamentary powers were obtained to construct a branch of 1¾ miles from Fort William to Banavie, on the Caledonian Canal.

The original directors of the West Highland were the Rt. Hon. Lord Abinger (Chairman), Cameron of Lochiel, Capt. R. W. Colquhoun, The Mackintosh and Robert Stewart, the Secretary being G. B. Wieland (then also Secretary of the North British). The Act provided that all the directors appointed therein should retire at the first meeting; three were re-elected, and the Marquis of Tweeddale and R. G. E. Wemyss replaced The Mackintosh and Robert Stewart, the Marquis of Tweeddale (then Chairman of the North British) being elected Chairman. Messrs. Formans & McCall of Glasgow were appointed engineers and the contract for construction of the new line, which was to extend from Craigendoran to Fort William, a length of 100 miles, was let to Messrs. Lucas & Aird of London.

The ceremony of cutting the first sod of the West Highland was performed by Lord Abinger near the Ben Nevis Distillery, Fort William, on 23rd October 1889. Mr. Aird, M.P., of the contractors, handed his Lordship a silver spade with which to carry out his task in the presence of a gathering of about 1,000 people. Work was commenced at Helensburgh, Arrochar, Crianlarich and Tyndrum, and on 3rd August 1894, the completed railway was finally inspected by the Board of Trade. Four days later, on 7th August, when the necessary sanction had been obtained, the West Highland was opened throughout for passenger traffic, so providing the first instance in this country of 100 miles of railway to be brought into use in one day.

The formal opening of the line took place on 11th August. A special train of ten carriages hauled by two locomotives left Glasgow at 8.15 a.m., conveying the Marquis of Tweeddale, accompanied by the Marchioness, directors of the West Highland and North British (by whom the line was to be worked and maintained) and some 250 other guests. Its arrival at a temporary platform outside Fort William station was greeted by cheers from a large crowd. Just ahead of the train had been erected a huge battlemented triumphal arch of heather, crowned with flags and medallions showing the arms* of the West Highland and North British

---

* The coat of arms of the West Highland, which was a replica of the Company's seal, is reproduced on the cover, together with the London & North Eastern heraldic device. It embraced the arms of Inverness (the Crucifix), Perth (the Paschal Lamb), Inveraray (herring entering net) and Dumbarton (elephant and tower), the county towns of the counties traversed by the line. The coat of arms of the North British, which contained the emblems of Edinburgh and Berwick, is illustrated on page 37.

Craigendoran signal box. Closed May 2, 1937.

Railways. A double gateway, similarly bedecked, within the arch kept closed the approach to the terminus of the line, the bolt securing the gate being made fast with a little gold padlock. This the Marchioness of Tweeddale duly unfastened and withdrew the bolt, and the train passed slowly through the gateway to the strains of the Marchioness of Tullibardine's March, played by a couple of pipers on top of the arch. In a spacious marquee nearby 400 people were then entertained to lunch, presided over by the Marquis of Tweeddale, the catering being in the hands of the North British Station Hotel, Glasgow. In the speeches that followed it was revealed by Mr. Aird that 2,000 to 5,000 men had been employed on the work, whilst Cameron of Lochiel, with representatives of the Caledonian and Highland Railways on either side of him as guests, remarked that courtesy forbade him referring to the opposition to the West Highland shown by these two companies! The ceremony over, the guests returned to Glasgow by their special train which, leaving Fort William at 4 p.m., made the journey in 5½ hours.

Before dealing with the events that led to the construction of two lines which extended the West Highland westwards and northeastwards, namely the Mallaig extension and Invergarry & Fort Augustus Railway, it is worth recording that one of the North British staff intimately associated with the early days of the West Highland was still alive when the line attained its Jubilee in 1944. He was Robert Beattie, of Fort William, who entered the service of the North British in 1884, and was a driver from the beginning of 1895 until he retired in 1931, the whole of his driving service of 37 years being spent on the West Highland. He was fireman on the first engine to run on any part of the new line when a locomotive was loaned to the contractors in February 1894 for hauling ballast trains from Craigendoran to Garelochhead, and was in the engine crew of the train by which the contractors and North British officials undertook the testing of bridges before the line was opened. Later he acted as fireman on the train that was run to convey the personnel who were to staff the new stations, and he was fireman on the empty carriage train of new bogie vehicles that ran to Fort William on 3rd August to form the first passenger train to run south to Glasgow four days later, when he was again fireman. Beattie drove the first fish train from Mallaig in 1901, after the extension to that place had been completed, and he was also the driver of the first one-day excursion to be run from Fort William to Glasgow. He died on 1st June 1945 at the ripe old age of 81.

Schemes for an alternative rail route to Inverness were by no means yet dead, and in the year before the West Highland was opened two were put forward, one by the Highland Railway, closely followed by another from the West Highland camp, but after much argument the two Companies agreed to withdraw their Bills. Two years later, in 1895, the West Highland and North British Railways introduced a Bill to extend the former from a point on the Banavie branch (opened on 1st June of that year), just outside Fort William, to Mallaig, a distance of 41 miles. The Highland again opposed the scheme, fearing that it would divert traffic from its route to Strome Ferry and menace its recently sanctioned extension to Kyle of Lochalsh. However, the Highland was eventually persuaded to withdraw its objection and received £500 for its Parliamentary expenses, the West Highland and North British agreeing not to promote, directly or indirectly, any railway through the Great Glen for at least ten years.

Arrochar & Tarbet local arriving at Craigendoran

Shandon station shortly after it was opened

In the following year, 1896, the West Highland Act was passed, authorising the extension from Banavie to Mallaig and the construction of a harbour at the latter place. The Government, recognising the value of the new line to the country through which it was to pass, and the small volume of traffic from which the Company could reasonably expect to recoup itself for its outlay, guaranteed for thirty years a dividend of 3 per cent upon £260,000, which was some £10,000 less than half the total cost of construction. The Government also agreed to contribute a further sum of £30,000 towards the cost of the pier and breakwater at Mallaig.

The comments of Mr. John Conacher, General Manager of the North British, regarding the development of the West Highland at this period, as recorded in an interview with the *Railway Magazine*

Goods train at Crianlarich hauled by class J39, No. 2979

Tyndrum Upper, with camping coach just visible through the trees.

in 1898, are of some interest. Of the Mallaig extension, he said : " The Treasury guarantee part of the capital with a view to the development of the fishing and crofting industries in the western districts and the Hebrides . . . The journey from Glasgow to Skye will be shortened by over 80 miles, while a much larger reduction will take place in the distances from the fishing grounds." Of future plans he remarked : " One must not talk of finality in railway enterprise. Parliament has already sanctioned the extension of the West Highland main line to Ballachulish, and the Light Railway Commissioners have now before them a scheme for a further extension from Arrochar to St. Catherine's on Loch Fyne, to serve Inveraray and develop the well-known fisheries on that loch." Unfortunately neither of these schemes matured and with the abandonment of the former project a useful link with the Caledonian at Ballachulish was lost.

The engineers for the Mallaig extension were Messrs. Simpson & Wilson of Glasgow and the contractors Messrs. Robert McAlpine & Sons, also of Glasgow, and on 21st January 1897, the first sod was cut at the village of Corpach by Lady Margaret Cameron of Lochiel. Operations were also commenced at four other points and although it was anticipated that the work would be completed early in 1900, various engineering difficulties arose and the line was not opened for traffic until 1st April 1901, the working and maintenance being undertaken by the North British Railway. The opening was carried out with little formality. The first train left Mallaig at 7.20 a.m., bringing passengers who had left Stornoway

Bridge of Orchy

Tulloch station (originally Inverlair) in 1914

Spean Bridge seen shortly after it was opened

the previous night, and reached Glasgow at 1.55 p.m. In the opposite direction a train left Edinburgh at 4.30 a.m. and Glasgow at 5.55 a.m., reaching Mallaig at 11.45 a.m. There the travellers were greeted with handshakes, congratulations and welcomes in Gaelic and English. Ten minutes later two steamers, the *Lovedale* and the *Clydesdale*, the former on the Portree and the latter on the Stornaway passage, cast off from Mallaig pier, and five minutes afterwards, at noon, the train left again for the south.

In 1896, the year the Mallaig extension was authorised, a local Company called the Invergarry & Fort Augustus Railway introduced a Bill to construct a line from Spean Bridge, on the West Highland, to Fort Augustus, a distance of 24 miles, leaving a gap of but 30 miles between the latter place and Inverness. After encountering considerable opposition, the Bill was passed on 14th August, and was destined to precipitate a greater Parliamentary struggle than ever between the Highland on the one hand and the West Highland and North British on the other. Despite the agreement of 1895, both sides put forward schemes in 1897 for the connecting link from Fort Augustus to Inverness, these to include running powers over the already authorised Invergarry & Fort Augustus Railway, which put forward its own proposal for an extension to Inverness. In the costly litigation that followed, in which each side fought to keep the other out of its territory, the preamble to the Highland Bill was proved by the Commons, only to be thrown out by the Lords.

Any hopes the Invergarry & Fort Augustus entertained of becoming part of what would have undoubtedly been an important cross-country link were therefore dashed, and it was left to proceed with the construction of its line from Spean Bridge to Fort Augustus. The engineers were Messrs. Formans & McCall and the contractor Mr. James Young of Glasgow. The works were finished towards the end of 1901, but by then the authorised capital, including loans, of £344,000 was exhausted, owing to the heavy engineering costs entailed, and no money was left for the purchase of locomotives and rolling stock. As, however, the line was physically connected with the West Highland at Spean Bridge, the North British was approached to work it, and this the Company was very willing to do—at cost price. In view of the light nature of the traffic anticipated for some years the offer was a fair one, but the directors of the Invergarry & Fort Augustus considered they should get better terms because their line served a district which two railways each regarded as its own to the exclusion of the other, and a personal guarantee by the North British directors was demanded. This was refused and the Invergarry & Fort Augustus thereupon offered its line to the Highland.

This action once more brought the North British and Highland Railways into conflict, and the Parliamentary battle that ensued

Early view of the original Fort William station

was as stormy as that of 1897. The opening of the line was inevitably delayed, as it was not until 30th June 1903 that the Highland obtained its Act to work the Invergarry & Fort Augustus for an annual payment of £4,000. Once again the Highland and North British entered into a compact to end further aggression upon each other's territory, the former promising never to try to penetrate nearer to Fort William and the latter giving a similar undertaking with regard to Inverness, an agreement which sounded the death knell of the connecting link between the latter city and Fort Augustus.

The old Banavie Pier station in 1913.

Looking east from Banavie station in 1914

The Invergarry & Fort Augustus line was passed by the Board of Trade on 14th July 1903, and eight days later the railway was opencd officially by Mrs. Ellice of Glengarry. Mr. Cunninghame, a director, presented her with a gold whistle with which to give the " right away " for the departure of the first train. As soon as Mrs. Ellice had blown the whistle the train moved off amidst cheers and the explosions of fog-signals. Stops were made at all stations, and upon arrival at Fort Augustus the guests took lunch, presided over by Mr. William Whitelaw, chairman of the Highland, who, during the course of a speech, reiterated that his Company had no

Glenfinnan station in the early days

17

intention of making a line from Fort Augustus to Inverness. He did, however, recognise that the Highland would not be free from responsibility in seeing that there was a good through connection between Inverness and the Invergarry & Fort Augustus line and the south. That connection was made by Messrs. David MacBrayne's steamers and he had no doubt that it would be satisfactorily maintained.

That Mr. Whitelaw's hopes were over-optimistic was apparent when two years later, in 1905, the Highland applied for powers to own and run their own steamboats on Loch Ness. MacBrayne, whose steamers held a monopoly on the northern part of the Caledonian Canal, strongly opposed the Bill, and the Invergarry & Fort Augustus Railway objected on the grounds that the steamer services proposed would enable the Highland to prevent them making any attempt to extend their line through the Great Glen. This combined opposition secured the defeat of the Bill.

Although the Highland had been authorised in 1903 to work the Invergarry & Fort Augustus for ten years, with the option of renewal, the sparse traffic, combined with the complete physical isolation of the line from the Highland system, soon induced them to withdraw in favour of the North British which, on 1st May 1907 took over the working of the railway for the next four years. In the same year, certain trains that during the summer months had hitherto run forward over a one mile extension to the Pier station at Fort Augustus, at which steamers called, were discontinued ;

Lochailort station

Fort August pier station, with Loch Ness stretching away behind

the service was never restored and the rails on the extension and station buildings at the pier were subsequently removed.

On 31st December 1908 the original section from Craigendoran to Fort William, the Banavie branch and the Mallaig extension, which altogether had cost about £2,370,000 to build, were absorbed by the North British Railway. Three years later, on 31st October 1911, the Invergarry & Fort Augustus Railway closed their line, but re-opened it on 1st August 1913, working being resumed by the North British which, in the following year, purchased the undertaking for £27,500. Twenty years later, on 1st December 1933, the London & North Eastern Railway, of which the North British was a constituent company, closed the Fort Augustus line to goods and passenger traffic. It was decided, however, to maintain the track and to run one freight train weekly, on Saturdays, to serve the depots at Gairlochy, Invergarry and Fort Augustus.

Fort August station in 1914

Arrangements were made for road motors to provide a goods and parcel service four times each way daily, and the Northern Scotland Traffic Commissioner granted licences for a bus service for passengers, four times daily, to be operated jointly by MacIntyre & Sons and Macrae & Dick.

In a letter to the author, Mr. William Whitelaw summed up his unique connection with the Invergarry & Fort Augustus in the following words : " As Chairman of the Highland I was responsible for opening it and then of closing it ; then of opening it again on behalf of the N.B. and finally of practically closing it—I suppose for ever—again ; but for the war perhaps the rails would have been lifted." He added : " I shall never forget my meeting with the Chairman and Secretary of the Invergarry Company when I settled the purchase price, including the Fort Augustus Hotel, at £27,000 for an undertaking which had cost nearly £350,000. Some day

Aberchalder station (1914)

I may have the pleasure of seeing you when I can tell you the details of that meeting . . . ! " To the lasting regret of the author, Mr. Whitelaw died before those undoubtedly entertaining details were divulged.*

The Fort Augustus line took on a new lease of life during the last war, as will be seen in Chapter V, and when in June 1946 it became known that its total closure was being considered a storm of public resentment broke upon the L.N.E.R. and Ministry of Transport. Protest meetings were held at Fort William and elsewhere and various bodies registered their strong disapproval. Once again advocates for the construction of the rail link between Fort Augustus and Inverness came forward and an Oban Councillor suggested the use of a light diesel car for passenger traffic. Eventually the Inverness Town Council sent a deputation, headed by Sir Donald Cameron of Lochiel, to interview the Minister of Transport.

But the heavy maintenance costs in relation to the quantity of traffic conveyed were too great, as a Kingussie timber merchant discovered when he planned early in 1947 to hire the line for the transport of timber from the Glenquoich area. Accordingly, acting upon instructions issued by the Ministry, the L.N.E.R. finally closed it on 31st December 1946. Driver Tim Brady of Fort William drove the last freight train but the last train of all was the optimistic timber merchant's one-coach " special ", which made a survey trip over the line on 28th March of the following year.

---

* Mr. William Whitelaw became Chairman of the North British in 1912 and of the London & North Eastern Railway upon its formation on 1st January 1923. His old company, the Highland, together with the Caledonian, became constituent companies of the London Midland & Scottish Railway. He retired on 30th September 1938, being succeeded by Sir Ronald W. Matthews, and died on 19th January 1946.

Ready for the off at Mallaig in the early days

Craigenarden viaduct on Loch Lomondside, shortly after construction

II—ENGINEERING FEATURES

The West Highland Railway traverses some of the loveliest mountain, moorland, river, glen and loch scenery in Scotland, and for the last ten miles into Mallaig the line skirts the Atlantic. For one-third of the way between Craigendoran and Fort William it was built through regions totally destitute of public roads and even today the only other way of seeing these regions is by walking. With the prospect of a sparse traffic for many years the West Highland was built as cheaply as possible, and sharp curves abound, the minimum radius south of Fort William being 11 chains (with one or two instances of short lengths of sharper curve), and on the Mallaig extension 10 chains. In *Mountain, Moor and Loch*, published in 1894, it was stated " There is no question that the line has been well engineered. When Mr. Charles Forman, whose scheme it is, had laid down his route from Craigendoran to Fort William, he was astonished to discover in some old Parliamentary papers that an almost identical course, for a turnpike road, had been traced in the beginning of the century by Telford, the famous engineer who constructed the Caledonian Canal. In one sense it was a curious coincidence, but more properly it might be said to be a voucher for the soundness of the plan, since two engineers had arrived independently at the same conclusions at different dates."

The original section from Craigendoran to Fort William has a ruling gradient of 1 in 50 and, together with the Banavie branch, was laid with double-headed rails of North British Railway pattern, weighing 75 lbs. per yard. An extraordinary feature was the absence of tunnels, there being originally only one, but 49 yards long,*

The first edition gave 47 yards.

between Arrochar and Ardlui ; west of Fort William, on the Mallaig extension, there are eleven, most of them quite short.   Throughout from Craigendoran to Mallaig and on the Banavie branch the line is single, except at passing places, and is controlled by electric train tablet apparatus.   Signals are of the usual North British Railway type, lower quadrant semaphores on lattice iron posts, now gradually being renewed with L.N.E.R standard upper quadrant arms.

Seventeen stations were built on the original section of the West Highland.   These were Craigendoran (the high level portion), Helensburgh (Upper), Row (later renamed Rhu), Shandon, Garelochhead, Whistlefield, Arrochar & Tarbet, Ardlui, Crianlarich, Tyndrum, Bridge of Orchy, Rannoch, Tulloch* (optimistically labelled " Tulloch for Kingussie," the latter being no less than 32 miles away and with a main line station of its own on the Highland

* Originally called Inverlair, the name being changed in January 1895.

Horseshoe bend at Auch between Tyndrum and Bridge of Orchy

Lattice girder viaduct by Rannoch station

Admiring the view on Nevis bridge, shortly after opening

Railway!), Roy Bridge, Spean Bridge and Fort William. The seventeenth station was the branch terminal Banavie, renamed Banavie Pier when the Mallaig extension station at Banavie was subsequently brought into use.

At all of these stations, save Whistlefield, passing loops were provided. There were also additional loops at Glen Douglas, Gortan (now spelled Gorton) and Corrour (the original Gaelic name of which was Lebruaridh), the last named now being a station, and the greatest length of line without a passing loop was between Corrour and Tulloch, 10 miles. Glen Douglas had a semi-private station for some time and has since become popular with hikers, trains being scheduled to call there for their benefit. No tickets are issued to or from Glen Douglas, travellers from the Glasgow direction having to book to Arrochar & Tarbet and those in the opposite direction to Whistlefield. Those joining at Glen Douglas obtain their tickets with the aid of the signalman, who asks Arrochar & Tarbet or Whistlefield, as the case may be, to send them on by the train on which the passengers intend to travel!

Fersit halt, south of Tulloch, was opened on 1st August 1931 for use by workmen engaged upon the Lochaber power scheme; it was closed on 31st December 1934. During the last war additional passing loops were installed or existing loops were extended at Craigendoran, Helensburgh (Upper), Rhu, Faslane junction (at which a new branch to Military Port No. 1 on Faslane Bay diverged), Spean Bridge and Mallaig junction, all of which are described in Chapter V. More recently, halts known as Faslane Junction, Inveruglas and Glen Falloch, together with a goods loop and three sidings at the second-named, have been provided for the transport of the Loch Sloy power scheme workers. Inveruglas was brought into use on 29th October 1945 and Glen Falloch and Faslane Junction on 10th April and 26th August respectively of the following year.

The stations on the West Highland do not differ materially in arrangement and the buildings are somewhat after the Swiss style. The lower courses of the walls are of fine facing brick in cement mortar, the upper parts being of timber faced with tapered wood shingles, the latter having been originally imported from Switzerland. With the exception of Rhu, Tulloch, Roy Bridge, Spean Bridge and Fort William, the stations are of the island platform type, connected with the entrances by 8-feet wide subways; an elevation and plan of a typical example are given in Appendix A. Craigendoran station consists of a high-level island platform for the West Highland line and a low-level station of two through platforms for the Helensburgh line together with a terminal bay on the adjoining pier; the physical connection between the Helensburgh line and the West Highland is effected at Craigendoran junction, 17 chains east of the station. The signalling of both

Snowshed at Cruach, north of Rannoch. South end, interior and north end

stations at Craigendoran is controlled from Craigendoran junction box, but there was a rather unusual elevated signal box that once performed this function, illustrated on page 10 ; it was closed on 2nd May 1937 and dismantled soon afterwards. The most important intermediate station is Crianlarich, which is connected with the Callander-Oban line of the former Caledonian Railway by a single track spur of 39 chains, still used regularly for the exchange of goods traffic between the L.N.E.R. and L.M.S. The original terminus, Fort William, possesses two platforms, one of them being double-faced.

All the steel bridges on the Craigendoran-Fort William section and on the Banavie branch were constructed by Messrs. Alexander Findlay & Co., of Motherwell, on behalf of the contractors, Messrs. Lucas & Aird, and, including cattle creeps, stream and occupation bridges, there were needed no less than 400 of them, 350 being viaducts and underbridges and 50 overbridges. Glen Falloch viaduct has the longest as well as the highest span, the 118 feet centre span being 144 feet above the bed of the stream ; it consists of lattice girder spans resting on granite piers and is typical of many others on the line. Some of the viaducts are on sharp curves and, in addition to the usual check rails, wheel guards on either side of the running rails are provided, to give further protection in the event of derailment. The longest viaduct is on the moor of Rannoch, where the line is carried for 684 feet over a depression on the moor in nine clear spans of 70 feet 6 inches, partly on a 12 chain radius. This viaduct was the largest on the line to be constructed with cantilever lifting tackle. Across Rannoch moor, a great boggy plain 1,000 feet above sea level and about 20 miles wide, the bed of the railway was cross-drained to take off the water, and a thick mattress of fascines composed of tree roots and brushwood laid down, on top of which were thrown excavations from other parts of the line, together with thousands of tons of ashes, until the whole was solid enough to allow the permanent way to be laid. On the Banavie branch the viaduct over the river Lochy, consisting of four 80 feet spans, is of particular interest because cast iron cylinders had to be sunk for the founding of the piers, whilst the floor of the structure is attached half way up the main girders, a form of construction that economises the wind bracing.

Reference must be made to four other features of engineering interest, namely, the snowshed in the Cruach rock cutting to the north of Rannoch station, the remotely-controlled level crossing gates at Fort William and the Lochaber and Loch Sloy power scheme diversions. The snowshed was built a few years after the opening of the line when it had been found that the cutting was susceptible to complete blockage from drifting during snowstorms, and it was, and still is, the only snowshed on a British railway.

Lochy viaduct on the original Banavie branch line

It is located in the deepest part of the cutting and is 205 yards long, being protected at each entrance by snow fences. The top of the rock being very uneven, dwarf concrete walls, 27 feet 6 inches apart, were constructed to a uniform height of 13 feet above rail level. The roof principals, placed at 6 feet centres, were built of old rails laid on the flat and curved to a radius of 38 feet, the portions of the rails resting on the concrete wall being bent level and bolted down to it. The corrugated iron roof is in three longitudinal portions and during the summer months the centre one is removed to reduce the effect of engine blast on the structure.

The level crossing with remotely-controlled gates is about 150 yards from Fort William signal box. Originally it was operated without wheel, cranks, rods or gear by a gatekeeper, and before the gates could be closed against the railway the signalman had to release them by pulling a lever interlocked with the signals. Since 1927, however, the gate movement has been made by an electric motor fed from the town mains and operated by the signalman by means of a hand switch electrically connected with the gates release lever and a lever which operates the stops mechanically. The gates are electrically detected in their two positions, the signalman having an indicator which shows if the gates are " for the railway " or " for the roadway." Road traffic is warned of the position and movement of the gates by two indicators and a loud sounding bell, the former showing " caution " when the gates are set for road traffic and " stop " when they are set for the railway. The bell rings for a short time before the gates are moved against the roadway.

The Lochaber power scheme called for a diversion of nearly 1½ miles of line alongside Loch Treig (from 78 m. 100 yards to 80 m. 175 yards) across one end of which a dam was built to allow the level of the loch to be raised about 35 feet, a portion of

Swing bridge at Banavie

the dam occupying the original route of the railway. The diversion is partly on embankment and partly in cutting, and entailed the construction of a tunnel 147 yards in length* and three underbridges. Under the diversion two water tunnels thread their way, one carrying water from Loch Laggan to Loch Treig, the tunnel in use being dependent on the level of Loch Treig. The work was started on 4th April 1931 and completed by 7th August of the following year, when the normal traffic which, until then had been maintained over the original route, was transferred to the new line. The diversion did not affect the total route mileage of the West Highland.

A diversion of lesser magnitude was required for the Loch Sloy power scheme. At Inveruglas the pipes carrying the water from Loch Sloy down to the power station had to pass below the railway, thus involving the construction of a new bridge. To avoid the imposition of a speed restriction and other difficulties, the L.N.E.R. diverted a ¼ mile of the line to a temporary embankment west of the site whilst the bridge was being built. The bridge is now in use and the diversion has been removed except for a portion at the north end, which has been retained as a siding for the handling of materials for the construction of high pressure pipe-lines.

The 1¾ miles Banavie branch which, as recorded in the previous chapter, was opened on 1st June 1895, terminated alongside the Caledonian Canal. It commenced at Banavie junction, which was laid facing Fort William, a mile distant. The Mallaig extension took off from the Banavie branch at a point slightly over a mile and a quarter from Banavie junction, the effect of this being to shorten the branch to less than half a mile. Banavie junction was at the same time renamed Mallaig junction and the point at which the Mallaig extension actually commenced became Banàvie junction.

---

* Recent remeasurement. The first edition gave 150 yards.

The 4.50 pm Fort William-Mallaig crosses Glenfinnan

In addition, as the Mallaig extension was to be provided with a station at Banavie, the branch terminal was renamed Banavie Pier.

The Mallaig extension has a ruling gradient of 1 in 40. Nine stations were built, these being at Banavie, Corpach, Lochielside, Glenfinnan, Lochailort, Beasdale (private station for Arisaig House), Arisaig, Morar and Mallaig, passing places being installed at Mallaig junction, which was laid out thus for the extension but not for the line to the south, and at Glenfinnan, Lochailort and Arisaig stations. The buildings are similar in character to those on the original West Highland section, apart from the fact that all are of the side platform type save at Mallaig, where a single island platform is provided, the track on the seaward side running out to the steamer pier in company with a second track which passes outside the station. During the war loops were laid in at Corpach and Camus-Na-Ha and these are referred to in more detail in Chapter V.

One of the problems encountered in building the Mallaig extension was that of obtaining labour, as the navvies were principally Irish and would not stay in the country for any lengthy period. In contrast to the original West Highland section, the transport of materials to the route of the line was easy; boats could be beached at any point along the first nine miles of route, and on

Loch Eil the contractors built a pier and a temporary line thence to the actual railway. Nevertheless, the proximity of Loch Eil had one disadvantage, as no less than seventeen sea-walls had to be provided between Corpach and Kinlocheil to protect the permanent way from the tidal waters of the loch, which can be very rough in stormy weather. Another great difficulty encountered was the amount of cutting in hard rock, which was responsible for much delay, and from the neighbourhood of Glenfinnan onwards to Mallaig there are many heavy rock cuttings and long embankments. Although it was originally planned to drive only two tunnels, it was eventually found necessary to increase that number to eleven, the longest of which is the 349 yards tunnel at Borrodale.*

In common with the Craigendoran—Fort William line, sharp curves, viaducts and bridges abound. Just beyond Banavie the Caledonian Canal is crossed by a swing bridge, illustrated on page 29 ; the Canal is not very wide at this point, and to avoid restricting the waterway by pivoting the bridge from a pier in midstream, it is pivoted at about a third of its length on a pier on one bank, and swings clear of the canal. Although a signal box called Banavie Canal Bridge was provided at the bridge, it was not a block post, the western approach being protected by Tomonie signal box and the eastern by Banavie Junction signal box. On 4th February 1912, however, the signal box at Canal Bridge became a block post and that at Tomonie was closed, and on 4th November nine years later Banavie Junction signal box ceased to operate as a block post, the junction points being controlled by a tablet locked ground frame, the tablet for this being held by Mallaig Junction signal box.

At Glenfinnan there is the stately, curved concrete viaduct that is probably the best-known engineering feature of the line. Glenfinnan viaduct is built on a 12 chain curve, is 416 yards in length and 100 feet high, and consists of 21 arched spans of 50 feet each ; it is

---

* The first edition gave 350 yards.

Lochailort rock cutting

both approached and quitted through rock cuttings. Lastly, there is the viaduct over Borrodale burn. This again is a concrete structure 86 feet in height and consisting of one span of 127 feet 6 inches and two of 20 feet ; at the time of its construction it was claimed to possess the longest concrete arch to be found on any railway in the world.

The Fort Augustus line, or Invergarry & Fort Augustus Railway, to give it its original title, starts from the West Highland at Spean Bridge, with which it forms a double junction at the west end of the station. The junction is laid in a trailing direction to Fort William, 9 miles distant. The line has a ruling gradient of 1 in 66, was equipped with 30 feet rails weighing 75 lbs. per yard, and is single throughout, except at passing places, although sufficient land was acquired for the provision of double track. Stations were built at Gairlochy, Invergarry, Aberchalder, Fort Augustus and Fort Augustus Pier, at all of which passing places (or run-round loops) were provided, whilst at Letterfinlay, a little more than eight miles from Spean Bridge, one further crossing place was installed, but so far as is known it was never brought into use and was subsequently dismantled. By the time the North British took over the working of the line, another station had been constructed at Invergloy, between Gairlochy and Invergarry, at which trains were stopped to take up and set down passengers as required. As previously related, the Pier station was later dismantled and some time after the advent of the L.N.E.R. the passing loops at Invergarry and Aberchalder were removed.

The design of the station buildings followed the Swiss style, as in the case of most of those on the West Highland, and consisted of a framework of wood on a stone base, the timber framing being faced with tapered wood shingles and painted in different colours. Gairlochy and Invergarry (with its private waiting room for use by the owner of Invergarry House) were provided with island platforms, and Invergloy, Aberchalder and the Pier station at Fort Augustus with single side platforms. The main station at Fort Augustus consisted of a side platform and a double-faced platform, one face of the latter being served by the through line to the Pier station, and the other face and the side platform by two terminal roads.

Messrs. Webb & Thomson's electric staff system was installed for controlling the line between Spean Bridge and Fort Augustus, with intermediate block points at Gairlochy and Invergarry, whilst the Pier line was worked by one engine in steam. Sidings at Invergloy and Aberchalder were secured by Annett's Lock, the key of which was attached to the electric staff of the appropriate section and, somewhat similarly, the lever controlling a swing bridge over the Caledonian Canal between the main and Pier stations at Fort Augustus was unlocked by an electric staff held in the signal box at the main station.

North end of Loch Oich tunnel (1914)

It would appear that somewhat different arrangements were in force when the line was first brought into use. According to Highland Railway Programme of Special Trains No. 271 for 19th–25th July 1903, the line was worked by electric train staff, with staff sections as follows :

Fort Augustus Pier—Fort Augustus
Fort Augustus—Invergarry
Invergarry—Gairlochy
Gairlochy—Spean Bridge

The siding points at Fort Augustus Pier and Aberchalder stations were controlled by staff locks, opened by means of the staff for the section in which they were located. Furthermore, it was laid down that the swing bridge would be left open for the canal after railway traffic ceased each weekday, and during Sundays, whilst it was stated that the bridge was interlocked with the train staff at Fort Augustus signal box and at the Pier station and could not be opened for the canal when the train staff was out at either of these places.

Tunnels are as scarce on the Fort Augustus line as on the original section of the West Highland, the solitary example being located near the end of Loch Oich, just beyond Invergarry House ; it was driven through hard schist rock and is only 60 yards in length. But of bridges the Fort Augustus line has its full measure. The first of note is across the Spean, a splendid lattice girder structure of four spans, two of 60 feet, one of 120 feet, and one of 50 feet, supported at a height of 80 feet above the river by masonry piers. Another bridge of the lattice girder type strides the river Gloy ;

it consists of one span of 100 feet and two of 50 feet each, carrying the line 60 feet above the bed of the river. Further on, across the Calder Burn, is a skew girder bridge of five spans, three of 56 feet 5 inches, one of 40 feet and one of 24 feet 5 inches, resting on 7 feet 6 inches diameter cylindrical caissons sunk in gravel and filled with concrete.

Between the two stations at Fort Augustus the line was carried across the Caledonian Canal by a swing bridge, already referred to, and over the River Oich by a steel lattice girder viaduct consisting of two centre spans of 100 feet each, approached each side by spans of 50 feet. The swing bridge was manually worked, the operation of swinging taking about four minutes, but after the service to the Pier station was discontinued it was kept permanently opened for the passage of ships. It consisted of a short arm of 31 feet 11½ inches, and a long arm with a skew end, giving 86 feet 5¼ inches and 78 feet 9 inches length of girders. When the bridge was opened for railway traffic it was supported at three points, namely, by a bearing at the end of the long arm, by another 6 feet 11 inches from the centre of the pivot on the long arm, and by a third at 29 feet 10 inches from the centre of the pivot on the short arm. Open and swinging to canal traffic, the weight of the bridge was carried on a centre pivot with a ring of steadying wheels running on a cast iron race. The Oich viaduct and the swing bridge were removed in 1941.

The route mileage of the West Highland system as a whole reached its highest peak during the middle of 1907, just after the North British had taken over the working of the Invergarry &

Oich viaduct, between Fort Augustus Main and Pier stations (1914)

Climbing hard on the West Highland

Fort Augustus Railway and just before the Pier extension of the latter fell into disuse. The route mileage was then nearly 165¾, made up as follows:

	Miles	Chains
Craigendoran junction—Fort William station ...	99	70
Crianlarich spur	0	39
Mallaig junction—Banavie junction	1	26
Banavie junction—Banavie Pier station	0	31
Banavie junction—Mallaig station	39	40
Mallaig station—Mallaig pier	0	10
Spean Bridge junction—Fort Augustus station...	23	13
Fort Augustus station—-Fort Augustus Pier station	0	73
Total ...	165	52

The summit of the system is at Corrour, 1,347 feet above sea level, as will be seen from the gradient diagrams given in Appendix B.

NB coat of arms

NBR class N 4-4-0 No. 695 as originally built

NBR class L 4-4-0 No.695 as rebuilt

NBR class M 4-4-0 No.479, later 1324, as rebuilt

Although to all outward appearances the West Highland line from Craigendoran to Fort William and the subsequent extension thence to Mallaig were integral parts of the North British, by whom both were always worked and maintained, specially designed locomotives and saloon coaches were introduced at the outset. Special composite brake carriages were also used for the through traffic to and from Edinburgh. One of the original saloon coaches may be seen in the photograph on page 24, and dimensioned diagrams of both 1st and 3rd class vehicles are given in Appendix C. Under the L.N.E.R. regime no special passenger stock has been built for the line, but a class of six locomotives—the K4 2-6-0—was designed exclusively for use on the West Highland in 1937.

At the time of the opening of the West Highland in 1894 Mr. Matthew Holmes was Locomotive Superintendent of the North British, and in the preceding year six 4-4-0 engines, numbered 693-698, were built at Cowlairs Works to his design for working passenger services on the line. The first three were stationed at Fort William shed (which was built on the walled site of the original fort) and the class was known as the " West Highland bogies." Six more of the same design—Nos. 55, 393, 394 and 699-701— were built in 1894 and two years later a further twelve followed— Nos. 227, 231, 232, 341-346 and 702-704—and some of each series were allocated to the West Highland line. Seven of these locomotives were still in existence when the L.N.E.R. was formed on 1st January 1923, having previously had their numbers altered by the North British, by whom they were officially designated class N. The L.N.E.R. redesignated them class D35 and their numbers were:

Original N.B.R. Number	Later N.B.R. Number	L.N.E.R. Number
55	1434	10434
342	1439	10439
345	1442	10442
696	1448	10448
697	1449	10449
701	1452	10452
704	1453	10453

Four were withdrawn in 1923 and another at the beginning of 1924, the class becoming extinct with the withdrawal of Nos. 10439 and 10448 in October of the same year. It must be recorded, however, that one of the class, No. 695, of the first six of 1893, was rebuilt in 1919 by Mr. W. P. Reid, Mr. Holmes' successor, and survived until 1943. This veteran engine, classed L after reconstruction by the North British and D36 by the L.N.E.R.,

Ex NBR class C 0-6-0 No. 9606, as rebuilt

by whom she was re-numbered 9695, worked regularly on the West Highland until she was withdrawn.

In the early years of the line the freight traffic was light and a single through train each way daily between Glasgow (Sighthill) and Mallaig, together with another from Glasgow to Fort William and back, were usually sufficient. Freight trains were frequently hauled by the passenger engines where unbalanced workings arose, but on other occasions the class C 0–6–0 of Mr. Holmes' design, of which large numbers were built between 1888 and 1900 for use throughout the North British system, was usually employed. In 1906, five years after the opening of the Mallaig extension, there appeared the first of Mr. Reid's class B 0–6–0 locomotives, and these soon began to displace the class C engines on the West Highland line. In the same year a new design of Mr. Reid's for hauling

NBR class B 0-6-0 No. 58

Ex-NBR class K superheated 4-4-0 No. 9885

some of the passenger trains made its debut. This was the
" Intermediate " class K 4-4-0, of which 12 were built, all eventually
being taken over by the L.N.E.R., by whom they were designated
class D32 and superheated between 1923 and 1926. Four years
later, in 1910, six 4-4-0 locomotives, originally constructed in
1877-1878 by Mr. D. Drummond (Mr. Holmes' predecessor)
and re-built between 1902 and 1904, were used for hauling passenger
trains on the West Highland from time to time. They were
designated class M and numbered 476-479 and 488-490. Nos.
476, 478 and 479, which were later re-numbered 1321, 1323 and
1324, survived until the days of the L.N.E.R., by whom they were
re-designated class D27. All three were withdrawn in 1923.

Experience gained with the " Intermediate " class K engines
led to the construction of the " Glen " class K 4-4-0, the first of

NBR class K 4-4-0 No.258 "Glen Roy"

41

which, designed by Mr. Reid, emerged from Cowlairs Works in 1913. Up to 1920 a total of 32 of these engines were built and some are still at work today on the West Highland. They became class D34 on the L.N.E.R. The next new type of locomotive to make its appearance was the class S superheated 0-6-0 freight engine, first built in 1914 to Mr. Reid's design: Altogether 104 locomotives of this class were constructed up to 1921 for main line freight train haulage on the North British, and some of them have done and are doing yeoman work on the West Highland line. They were designated class J37 by the L.N.E.R.

The first new type to appear in regular working after the formation of the L.N.E.R. was the class K2 2-6-0 mixed traffic locomotive of former Great Northern Railway design. Some of these engines were permanently transferred to Scotland in 1925 followed by a further batch between 1931 and 1932, and since the latter year all have been fitted at Cowlairs with side window cabs. Two years later, in 1934, those that were allocated to work on the West Highland were named after Lochs, as follows :

4674	Loch Arkaig	4693	Loch Shiel
4682	Loch Lochy	4697	Loch Quoich
4684	Loch Garry	4698	Loch Rannoch
4685	Loch Treig	4699	Loch Laidon
4691	Loch Morar	4700	Loch Lomond
4692	Loch Eil	4701	Loch Laggan
4704	Loch Oich		

The K4 2-6-0 locomotives followed in 1937. As previously mentioned, six were built, their numbers and names being :

3441	Loch Long
3442	The Great Marquess
3443	Cameron of Locheil
3444	Lord of the Isles
3445	MacCailin Mor
3446	MacLeod of MacLeod

In 1945, during Mr. Edward Thompson's regime as Chief Mechanical Engineer, No. 3445 became one of the "guinea pigs" in the L.N.E.R. locomotive standardisation scheme then being developed. Her three cylinders $18\frac{1}{2}$ inches in diameter by 26 inches stroke were replaced by two cylinders 20 inches in diameter by 26 inches stroke and she was given a boiler pressure of 225 lbs per square inch instead of 180 lbs. The conversion reduced the total weight of engine and tender in working order from 112 tons 12 cwts. to 111 tons 1 cwt. and the tractive effort from 36,598 lbs. to 32,081 lbs. No. 3445 is now designated K1 and is the prototype of one of the standard L.N.E.R. locomotive classes for mixed traffic duties.

Immediately prior to the war the passenger services were being worked with the K2, K4 and D34 locomotives already described.

NBR class S 0-6-0 No. 8

NBR class M 4-4-2T No. 102

NBR class L 4-4-2T

Ex GNR class H3 2-6-0 No. 4701 "Loch Laggan", as originally built

The local trains to and from Arrochar & Tarbet (referred to later) were sometimes hauled by ex-North British classes L (superheated) and M 4-4-2 tank engines of Mr. Reid's design (L.N.E.R. classes C16 and C15 respectively) and sometimes by L.N.E.R. class V1 2-6-2 tank engines, the first of which was constructed in 1930. The freight traffic was also handled by the K2 and K4 types, assisted by some J37 and J39 locomotives, the latter being a power-ful 0-6-0 freight design that first appeared on the L.N.E.R in 1926. Shunting was done by the train engines, except at Fort William, where J36 locomotives were employed, the same engines also running the ballast trains. Since the war the changes that have taken place have included the introduction of two class V4 2-6-2 engines, built 1941 and the last design of the late Sir Nigel Gresley, and the occasional use of B1 4-6-0 locomotives for the passenger

LNER class V1 2-6-2T No. 2900

LNER class K4 2-6-0 No. 3441 "Loch Long"

services. The J39 engines have been withdrawn for duties elsewhere and O7 2-8-0 ex-Government locomotives have been employed for freight train haulage between Glasgow and Fort William, these having first appeared during the war years, when they gave invaluable service.

On the Fort Augustus line the skeleton service since the beginning of December 1933 has generally been worked by a J36 engine, but in the early days and until the end of April 1907 the locomotive power was, of course, provided by the Highland. A diminutive 4-4-0 tank engine, No. 52, with *The Highland Railway* boldly inscribed on its sides, was usually to be found at the head of a train of three coaches that ran between Fort Augustus and Spean Bridge. This locomotive was one of three built in 1893 by Dübs & Co. which were similar to, although slightly heavier than, two other

LNER class V4 2-6-2 No. 3401 "Bantam Cock"

engines built by the same firm in 1891, all of them intended for the Uruguay Eastern Railway. Probably owing to some financial difficulties they never went overseas and the five engines were purchased by the Highland Railway, on which it is understood they were quite incorrectly dubbed "Yankees." No. 52, which until 1900 was numbered 15, had 16 inch by 22 inch cylinders, 5 feet 3 inches diameter coupled wheels, 3 feet diameter bogie wheels, a tank capacity of 900 gallons, a boiler pressure of 140 lbs. per square inch and weighed 42 tons 10 cwts in working order.*

Another locomotive to work on the Invergarry & Fort Augustus was 4–4–0 No. 48, built in 1901 at the Lochgorm Works of the Highland, and the last of a class known as the "Skye Bogies," designed by Mr. David Jones, the Locomotive Running Superintendent. Cylinders were 18 inches by 24 inches, coupled wheels 5 feet 3 inches diameter and bogie wheels 3 feet 2½ inches diameter. The boiler pressure was 150 lbs per square inch, the engine weighing 43 tons and the tender 30 tons in working order. No. 48, however, was not completed until after her designer had resigned, and in consequence was fitted with a chimney of the type standardised by his successor, Mr. P. Drummond.

Curiously enough, engines of the latter's brother, Mr. D. Drummond, heralded the advent of the North British, for two little 4–4–0 tank engines, Nos. 19 and 74, built to his design in 1882, were sent to the Fort Augustus line when the working changed hands. During the summer these locomotives had to haul five coaches and a through coach from Glasgow, and in winter a single West Highland bogie composite, seating twelve 1st and twenty-five 3rd class passengers. Incidentally, these tank engines were the

---

* *Railway Magazine.* Vol. 72, p. 199.

Ex-NBR class R 4-4-0T No.10456 formerly No. 74 and later No. 1456

Fort Augustus station back in 1903.

last class to be designed by Mr. Drummond for the North British, as it was in 1882 that he took up a similar appointment in the rival Caledonian camp and was succeeded by Mr. Holmes.   Locomotives Nos. 19 and 74 subsequently had their numbers altered by the North British to 1454 and 1456 respectively, and in company with twenty-eight similar engines were duly taken over by the L.N.E.R., when their numbers had 9000 added to them.   Designated class R on the North British, they became class D51 on the L.N.E.R.   During the last years of the passenger services C15 engines worked the branch, one of them being No. 9155 (N.B.R. No. 155).

Leading particulars of the North British and London & North Eastern locomotives that have regularly worked on the West Highland, the Mallaig extension and the Fort Augustus line are given in Appendix D.

Snow-bound near Glen Douglas in 1940

Banavie junction in 1914

IV—TRAIN SERVICES AND OTHER FEATURES

When the original section of the West Highland was opened on 7th August 1894 the passenger service consisted of three trains each way, leaving Glasgow (Queen Street High Level) at 7.30 a.m., 12.42 p.m. and 4.50 p.m., arriving Fort William at 12.15 p.m., 5.20 p.m. and 9.40 p.m. respectively, and departing from Fort William at 6.10 a.m., 11.15 a.m. and 4.25 p.m., reaching Glasgow at 11.00 a.m., 4.00 p.m. and 9.08 p.m. Through carriages between London (King's Cross), Edinburgh and Fort William were included on the 7.30 a.m. down and 4.25 p.m. up trains during the summer months only. This service was continued until 1st November 1894, when one train each way was withdrawn, the trains remaining being from Glasgow (Queen Street High Level) at 7.55 a.m. and 3.50 p.m., arriving Fort William at 12.47 p.m. and 8.47 p.m. respectively, and from Fort William at 7.20 a.m. and 3.55 p.m., reaching Glasgow at 12.25 p.m. and 8.43 p.m.

In the same year local trains serving intermediate stations between Craigendoran and Garelochhead were operated during the period June to October, there being four each way. Later this local service, the only one of its kind on the West Highland, was extended to Arrochar & Tarbet, the service consisting today of three trains each way, with an extra one on Saturdays, generally provided by a " push and pull " unit, for which C15 engine No. 9135 was fitted with vacuum control apparatus in 1940.

In 1895 a through train was introduced during the period June to September, leaving Edinburgh at 7.10 a.m. and arriving Fort William at 1.20 p.m., whilst in the return direction departure was made at 2.45 p.m. from Fort William, reaching Edinburgh at 9.23 p.m., an arrangement which was continued through the summer months until 1899. Two years later, when the line had been extended to Mallaig, the services were increased, and through carriages between King's Cross and Mallaig were introduced in the summer timetable. Of the services then run in the down direction, the 5.50 a.m. Glasgow to Mallaig, 3.45 p.m. Fort William to Mallaig and 4.50 p.m. Glasgow to Fort William were still identifiable in September 1939, although they had been re-timed. In the up direction, the 1.20 p.m. and 2.20 p.m. Mallaig to Glasgow and 4.20 p.m. Fort William to Glasgow were similarly recognisable in the 1939 services. Of the remaining original down services, the 7.15 a.m. Glasgow to Mallaig was discontinued in 1914, and it was not until 1929 that a second morning service was restored, this being the 4.28 a.m. through train from Edinburgh; the 12.45 p.m. Glasgow to Fort William, withdrawn in 1915, was restored in 1919 as the 11.23 a.m. Glasgow to Mallaig; the 8.30 p.m. Saturdays only train from Fort William to Mallaig was put on in 1925; while the 8.15 p.m. Saturdays excepted train commenced in 1930. The 7.06 a.m. Glasgow to Mallaig was a special timing which operated for only two months at the beginning of the last war. In the up direction, the 6.25 a.m. Mallaig to Glasgow was replaced

Tickets from the short-lived Invergarry & Fort Augustus Railway

by the 6.35 a.m. Mallaig to Fort William in 1916 ; the 7.35 a.m. Fort William to Glasgow was withdrawn in 1904, and the 5.50 a.m. Fort William to Glasgow in 1913 ; whilst the 8.10 a.m. Mallaig to Glasgow was introduced in 1913 and the 6.20 p.m. Mallaig to Fort William in 1904.

Sleeping cars first appeared on 22nd July 1901, these being attached to the 8.15 p.m. from King's Cross, which arrived at Fort William at 9.43 a.m., and to the return train which left at 4.20 p.m. and reached King's Cross at 7.10 a.m. The cars were run during the summer months only, an arrangement which continued until 1914, when the period was extended from May to October. Two years later the sleeping cars were withdrawn, but were resumed in 1919, and from April of the following year were retained on Fridays in the down direction and on Mondays in the up direction throughout the remainder of the year. In October 1929 sleeping cars commenced to run daily throughout the year, an arrangement which was continued until 2nd October ten years later, when the war brought an end to the service. The experiment of running sleeping cars from Mallaig was made in 1901, but it was dropped in the time-tables of the following year and has never since been resumed.

On the Banavie Pier branch passenger trains were run to and from Fort William in connection with steamers on the Caledonian Canal. In the summer of 1939 this train service consisted of one trip from Banavie Pier to Fort William on Mondays, Wednesdays and Fridays and one in the reverse direction on Tuesdays, Thursdays and Saturdays. The service ceased with the Saturday run to Banavie Pier on 2nd September 1939 and has not yet been restored, but the branch remains open for freight traffic.

On the Invergarry & Fort Augustus Railway the Highland introduced a daily service of four trains as shown below, save during the first week of operation, when all but the first up and last down trains served the Pier station.*

			a.m.	a.m.	p.m.	p.m.
Fort Augustus Pier station	dep		—	—	2.20	7.05
,, ,, station	...	,,	7.25	10.55	2.25	7.10
Aberchalder	... ...	,,	7.34	11.04	2.34	7.19
Invergarry	... ...	,,	7.49	11.16	2.46	7.31
Gairlochy	... ...	,,	8.21	11.46	3.16	8.01
Spean Bridge	... ...	arr	8.30	11.55	3.25	8.10
			a.m.	p.m.	p.m.	p.m.
Spean Bridge	... ...	dep	9.35	12.15	5.30	9.25
Gairlochy	... ...	,,	9.44	12.24	5.42	9.34
Invergarry	... ...	,,	10.14	12.54	6.15	10.04
Aberchalder	... ...	,,	10.26	1.06	6.27	10.16
Fort Augustus station	...	arr	10.35	1.15	6.40	10.25
,, ,, Pier station		,,	—	—	6.45	—

* Highland Railway Programme of Special Trains No 271 for 19th/25th July 1903.

NBR class C 0-6-0 No. 648 fitted with wooden snow plough

Ex-G.N.R. class H3 2-6-0 No. 4699 "Loch Laidon" fitted with steel snow shield

"Karrier" road-railer introduced in 1934 – the best of both worlds

Sleeping van for the use of permanent way staff

When the North British took over the working of the line on 1st May 1907, two services were given each way between Spean Bridge and Fort Augustus, being increased to four each way during the period July to September. The service was continued on much the same basis until 31st October 1911, when the line was closed, and upon it being re-opened on 1st August 1913, three trains daily each way were provided, these being reduced to two between October 1913 and May 1914. In July 1914, the summer service was strengthened by additional Monday, Wednesday and Saturday trains, the latter being a through service from Fort William to Fort Augustus, the Monday and Wednesday trains giving a like facility in the reverse direction, an arrangement which later developed into a daily through train to and from Fort William throughout the year. During 1916 and 1917 services were curtailed owing to the war, and as from May 1919 were resumed on a basis similar to those in operation four years earlier. Except for a reduction to three summer services each way as from 1921, there were no further alterations, apart from retimings, up to the time the line was closed for passenger traffic, namely on 1st December 1933.

Sunday train services have never been provided continuously throughout the year on the West Highland system, but a service of half-day excursions, first from Glasgow and later from Edinburgh as well, was advertised throughout the summer of 1934 and continued up to the outbreak of war. These excursion trains included restaurant cars which, incidentally, were first introduced on 8th July 1929 on the 4.30 a.m., 5.45 a.m. and 11.23 a.m. down, and 12.10 p.m., 4.05 p.m. and 5.12 p.m. up trains. They were run

Loco shed and turntable at Mallaig in 1914

53

throughout the summer, but during the remainder of the year only the 5.50 a.m. down and 4.05 p.m. up trains between Glasgow and Fort William were so equipped. From 11th September 1933 a restaurant car was attached to the 3.43 p.m. Glasgow to Fort William, returning from the latter place by the 8.35 a.m. from Mallaig to Glasgow, a facility which was available throughout the year until September 1939. On the outbreak of war, the restaurant car services were withdrawn from 2nd October 1939 but on the 4th of the following December one was restored, working on the 5.50 a.m. Glasgow to Fort William and returning from the latter place on the 8.25 a.m. ex Mallaig to Glasgow. In May 1942, the return working was transferred, as from Fort William, to the 1.00 p.m. from Mallaig, and the service was completely withdrawn on 5th April 1944. The full service was restored in the summer of 1946.

It should be recorded that prior to the appearance of restaurant cars on the line, refreshment baskets had been obtainable at Arrochar & Tarbet from 1st November 1894, for passengers from London and other places in England on notice being given to the guard at Craigendoran. This facility was extended to Crianlarich in the following July and in 1901, with the opening of the Mallaig extension, baskets were also made available at Fort William and Mallaig. These arrangements were continued until the restaurant cars came, and thereafter baskets were supplied only at Crianlarich where, on the platform, there still remains a huge notice board bearing the words " Refreshment Rooms. Luncheons, Teas and Dinners served. Time allowed by trains "—a reminder of the times before meals were obtainable on the trains.

The rather scanty freight train services in the early days of the West Highland, already referred to, began to increase by 1920, and later the Lochaber power scheme brought more traffic. There are now five freight trains each way daily between Glasgow and Fort William and one each way between the latter place and Mallaig. In addition, fish specials are run regularly from Mallaig during the greater part of the year.

Train services have been badly disorganised on several occasions owing to snowstorms, and more than once Tulloch station, for instance, has been completely obliterated. There were bad storms in 1902, 1906, 1908 and 1909, when trains or engines were totally snowed up for several hours. One of the worst snowstorms occurred in 1940, between 28th January and 9th February, when six miles of the line from south of Whistlefield to north of Glen Douglas were completely blocked. A double-headed plough was snowed-up midway, and an engine sent to its assistance shared a similar fate south of Glen Douglas. Subsequent drifts, coupled with a train of empty coaches becoming snowbound north of Helensburgh (Upper) did not make the work of clearance any easier and it was not until Friday 9th February, that the line could be re-opened for goods traffic, the passenger trains resuming on the 12th. The snow storm of 13th–16th March 1947 was even worse. During a single night snow drifts derailed vehicles at six different places between Shandon and Glen Douglas. Conditions were so severe that two members of the breakdown squad became frost bitten and only by bringing into play the maximum force that could be collected was the line cleared.

It is not surprising, therefore, that the Western District of the L.N.E.R. Scottish Area, in which the West Highland is included, should have more snow ploughs allocated to it than any other, there being two of the double type and fourteen of the single type distributed amongst the locomotive depots* in the district. All the ploughs are of steel, the old wooden type being illustrated on page 51 together with the modern steel snow shield. Nor, in view of the isolation of the central section of the line from the outside world, is it surprising to find sleeping vans provided for the permanent way maintenance staff; one of these useful vehicles is illustrated on page 52.

Another feature of particular interest from the maintenance point of view is the " road-railer." Prior to 1934 the L.N.E.R. had employed road lorries and rail motor trollies for permanent way work, but in that year the advantages of both were combined by the introduction of a 2-ton road-rail motor built by Karrier Ltd. of

---

* The only locomotive depot on the West Highland is at Fort William and this is in process of modernisation. There is, however, a locomotive shed at Mallaig, those at Crianlarich and Spean Bridge having been out of use for many years.

Loco shed, Fort William in 1914

Tribute to Mr Renton, one of the backers of engineers Lucas & Aird, Rannoch

Huddersfield, and illustrated on page 52. The road wheels are raised and lowered by crank action and transference from rail to road is effected by lowering them fully and running the vehicle on to a rail-level ramp, so lifting the flanged wheels clear of the metals. To reverse the process, the vehicle is driven slowly along the ramps until the flanged wheels drop into position on the rails. The sphere of operations of the road-railer is from Crianlarich northwards, using the road from that point to Bridge of Orchy, thence the railway to Tulloch and back to the road again from that place to Fort William. It is also run as a rail vehicle only on the Mallaig extension and its use has relieved rail traffic congestion by the elimination of ballast engine workings.

For many years the waiting rooms at Roy Bridge and Rannoch stations have been used each alternate Sunday afternoon for religious services. At the former the Church of Scotland Minister or his Assistant from Spean Bridge conducts the service and in the case of Rannoch the Minister travels from Bridge of Gaur, six miles away. The waiting room at Roy Bridge has also been the scene of a Sale of Work in aid of Belford Hospital, Fort William on at least one occasion.

Finally, there is the school at Gorton. Until Easter of 1938 a morning and afternoon train stopped specially at Gorton signal box to take children of the staff there to and from school at Rannoch. This school became overcrowded, and so the L.N.E.R. provided a carriage body by Gorton signal box and fitted it up with chairs and desks. A teacher was appointed by the educational authorities of the Argyll County Council, and from then until this day lessons in the three " R's " have been given in what surely must be one of the most unusual schools in Great Britain . . . one, moreover, in which there's a fourth " R " . . . Railways !

Roll call in the school-on-the-platform at Gorton

Military Port No. 1 at Faslane during the war

V—THE WEST HIGHLAND IN WARTIME

In the first edition of this book, published in 1944, it was stated on pages 15 and 17 ". . . During recent years an additional passing place has been laid in at Faslane junction, midway between Rhu and Shandon, where a private siding diverges." Again, on page 20, was the remark ". . . During recent years one more passing place has been made at Camus-Na-Ha, between Banavie and Corpach." Some private siding . . . some passing place! For security reasons it could not then be revealed that the former was the branch to Military Port No. 1 at Faslane and that the latter formed part of traffic facilities provided for the naval repair base at Corpach.

The part played by the West Highland during the war years is indicated by the movement of wagons over its lines. During 1938 26,743 loaded wagons were forwarded and received; in 1943 the figure was 68,565 and in the following year 90,327. The empty wagon movements also increased by leaps and bounds: in 1938, 19,822, in 1943, 44,049 and in 1944, 65,961. Although the passenger train service was curtailed—indeed part of the West Highland was in a prohibited area—the reduction was more than offset by the special trains operated to handle the large influx of service personnel and equipment. During 1943, for instance, 199 special trains were run to convey 2,142 officers and 45,774 other ranks.

Necessary adjuncts to the wartime traffic facilities on the West Highland were the construction of new marshalling yards at Ardmore, between Cardross and Craigendoran, and additional sidings at Craigendoran. At the former place an up yard for eastbound traffic and empties, consisting of a reception loop accommodating 100 wagons and nine sidings holding 406 wagons, and a down yard for loaded traffic to Faslane, comprised of a reception loop holding 150 wagons and nine sidings with a capacity of 406 wagons, were built. The layout included two new signal boxes, with accommodation for yard staff, and was first in operation on 28th February 1943. In the previous year, on 24th May, an independent group of nine sidings, adjoining the Ardmore new down yard and holding 250 wagons, was brought into use. This yard handled Admiralty traffic in connection with anti-submarine boom defence measures.

At Craigendoran extra siding accommodation for 200 wagons was provided north of the existing carriage sidings and two loops for trains travelling each way between Craigendoran East and the West Highland line at Craigendoran junction were laid in on the north side of the main line, together with a new signal box. A new yard, capable of holding 408 wagons in eleven sidings, was also provided slightly further east, this again being on the north side of the main line. These works were completed on 4th January 1942.

Inveruglas station

A locomotive turntable was installed in November of the same year. This is 70 feet in diameter, vacuum-operated and capable of turning any class of engine in the district in just over two minutes ; two storage tanks containing a reserve of power were provided to operate the turntable when a locomotive not fitted with the vacuum system has to be turned.

Although Craigendoran Pier is not part of the West Highland, it is situated by the southern extremity of the line and the use to which it was put during the war years is worth recording in these pages. In normal times the headquarters and starting point of the L.N.E.R. Clyde steamer services, Craigendoran Pier became one of the Clyde emergency ports set up in 1940 owing to the vulnerability of East Coast ports to air attacks. Berths were provided for discharging cargoes from shallow draught vessels which ferried the goods from ocean-going vessels lying in mid-river and electric trolleys carried the goods from the pier to rail vehicles alongside the passenger station pier platform. Barges from English canals, Dutch *schuyts* escaped from Holland and dockers and trolleys from London's " blitzed " Victoria Docks were all engaged in the work. The first cargo came ashore on 11th October 1940 and from that date until December of 1944 the barges, idle only when the water was too rough, made 4,280 journeys between ship and shore, landing over 170,000 tons of traffic, all of which went forward by rail.

Returning to the West Highland proper, the two stations after Craigendoran were given additional facilities to cope with the traffic to and from Faslane. At Helensburgh (Upper) the loops were extended and the signal box replaced by a new structure, these being brought into use on 21st December 1941. At Rhu a new passing loop and signal box were made available on 6th July of the same year and the up platform again brought into use, the original loop at this place having been removed some years before the war.

The old Glen Falloch station

At Faslane junction, at which a halt has now been built for the Loch Sloy power scheme workers, as mentioned in Chapter II, diverges a double line of about 2½ miles to Faslane, once a quiet bay on the Gareloch, which was converted into a port capable of accommodating a 35,000 ton battleship.   Military Port No. 1, as it was designated, was equipped with six berths each 500 feet long with 30 feet of water at low tide.   A wharf 1,500 feet in length, for dealing with vessels of shallow draught, such as lighters, was also provided.   The dock had a standage capacity of 1,700 wagons.

The line from Faslane junction to Military Port No. 1 was constructed by the War Department, has a falling gradient of 1 in 50 over most of its length and was laid with 75 lbs. flat bottom rails. Its working was performed by War Department staff and locomotives (of which there were eleven) on Continental principles, the object being to familiarise army personnel with the systems which would be encountered when D-Day had become a *fait accompli*. At Faslane junction exchange sidings holding 298 wagons were installed, these consisting of seven double-ended roads, three being for outwards traffic, three for inwards traffic and the remaining one for " run-round " purposes.   A new signal box, which was brought into operation on 27th April 1941, controlled access to the exchange sidings and buildings were also provided for L.N.E.R. staff, including the agent and his clerks.

The exchange sidings were first used for traffic in May 1942 and on the 27th of that month the first vessel to use Military Port No. 1 arrived to discharge old boom defence material.   The port was not quite finished and normal military traffic did not start passing until July.   From then onwards there was a steady flow of tanks, mobile cranes, heavy guns, motor launches, bulldozers, tractors, road rollers and even midget submarines.   During the period 1942– August 1945 Faslane exchange sidings received 104,877 loaded wagons and forwarded 8,022, a disparity which involved the L.N.E.R. in considerable return working of empty wagons.

A platform was provided at the end of the branch to deal with military and other special trains and the first passenger train entered the port on 5th August 1943, when Mr. Winston Churchill and others embarked on a transatlantic voyage.   From then, until the end of August 1945, 63 more through passenger trains were run.

The operation of the branch and of Faslane port itself has now been taken over by Metal Industries Ltd and considerable traffic is anticipated from shipbreaking activities there.   The maintenance of the branch and exchange sidings is now performed by the L.N.E.R. by arrangement with Metal Industries Ltd.

The next station where increased traffic brought about by the war demanded additional facilities was Spean Bridge, the junction for Fort Augustus.   Here a loop holding 52 wagons, together with an adjoining siding of 30 wagons capacity, were laid in at the entrance to the branch and two other sidings accommodating 14 and 27 wagons were constructed parallel to the up platform. The military authorities regarded the Fort Augustus branch as a reserve line of communication for the movement of troops should other routes become blocked and the facilities at Spean Bridge were designed for expeditious working in the· event of such an emergency, additional sidings also being provided at Fort Augustus itself.

Happily, other factors led to the temporary rejuvenation of the Fort Augustus line. A Commando training camp was set up at Achnacarry and a naval ammunition store established at Fort Augustus, but the biggest factor of all was the timber felled in the neighbouring forests by lumberjacks from Newfoundland. In 1943 the once-weekly freight train service was doubled and was further increased in the following year. By 1st May 1944 the volume of traffic demanded a goods train daily, almost entirely for the movement of timber.

The remaining wartime traffic facilities on the West Highland were provided on the Mallaig extension. First, at Mallaig junction, three dead-end sidings were looped-up throughout and connected to the Mallaig line ; then in November 1943 four new sidings were laid in immediately east of the converted loops and in February of the next year two more sidings were provided. The wagon standage capacity at Mallaig junction was thereby raised to 182 and gave welcome relief to Fort William which, with limited yard accommodation, was dealing with huge increases in aluminium and coal traffic and considerable ammunition traffic.

Lastly, the creation of a naval repair base at Corpach called for additional facilities at three places. West of the station the Admiralty constructed two looped sidings, each holding 26 wagons and connected at both ends to the Mallaig line. The first portion of the sidings, used for discharging materials for the construction of the naval base, was opened on 15th March 1942 and the layout was completed on 26th March of the following year.

The limited housing available in the Corpach district was quite insufficient to accommodate the personnel attached to the naval base and it was decided to erect two hundred concrete houses on the former Corpach golf course for the workmen and their families, numbering in all about 700. A siding holding 12 wagons was accordingly provided near the site for the discharge of 6,000 tons of building materials and soon a new community, known as Annat village, had been born. Most of the inhabitants were employees from naval dockyards in the south of England, with a few from Rosyth, and their transfer to Annat called for some 200 household removals by rail, all but five of which were handled in April 1943.

To enable the new sidings west of Corpach and at Annat to be worked efficiently, however, it was necessary to break the long single line section of 16 miles between Mallaig junction and Glenfinnan. This was done by constructing a loop accommodating 2 locomotives, 38 wagons and a van at Camus-Na-Ha, slightly more than 4¼ miles from Mallaig junction. A new signal box, controlling both the new loop and the sidings already described, was brought into use on 15th November 1942. Although the loop was not equipped for passenger train working, it was used to refuge freight trains on 283 occasions during 1943, saving them 83 hours delay monthly.

Many other places on the West Highland felt the impact of war. At Arrochar & Tarbet the tonnage of traffic dealt with was quadrupled and heads of livestock handled rose from 5,000 in 1938 to nearly 13,000 in 1944. The little wayside station at Bridge of Orchy forwarded 309 more loaded wagons in 1943 than it did in a peacetime year. Glenfinnan and Lochailort stations, which served a region used as a toughening and training ground for Commando forces, received long distance troop trains from all over the country. And at Mallaig, the Atlantic terminal of the line, imports and exports through the L.N.E.R. harbour jumped from 11,000 to 25,000 tons, less than 2 per cent of which was not rail-borne.

Water column and signal at Garelochhead

These achievements were performed on a railway which abounds with stiff gradients and sharp curves . . . above all, on a railway which is essentially a single track system. The officers and staff of the L.N.E.R. who administer, operate and maintain the West Highland may, with every justification, look back with pride on a job superbly done.

The Rannoch Line

follows the route of the
West Highland railway
across Rannoch Moor, from
Crianlarich as far as
Fort William

Another Famedram railway guide